I am

_____

This is my book.

My Feelings Matter

by

Ryan Lynn

Book Design and Production by Contact Lynn's Publishing
Front Cover Design by Tori Lynn

Contact Lynns Publishing
TheLynnses.com
214-997-4077

Thank you

To my Heavenly Daddy, thank you for Saving us and Loving us and Teaching us and taking care of us. You Are Awesome.

To my Grandmama K and Granddaddy J and my aunties K and A, thank you for always loving us and our mommy. I love you so much.

Great-grandma Mae H. Ponds, Thank you for loving on us and trying to teach big people, "Children are people too, they're just in little bodies." RIH

Thank you to Kim Wesson (Autumn, Jalen), Mr. Cris McFadden, Acting Coach Mr. Larome Armstrong, Cousins Charles and Taiwannika Walker (Tai'Charle, Braeden, Cameron), Mr. Isaac Lee, Ms. LaFonda (Michelle, Maria), Mr. Andy Brown, Ms. Michelle Davis (Parker, Hunter), Mr. Kelvin Edwards, Mrs. Skipper, Mrs. Summer, and Imogene (RIH) for the great things you've done for us.

Thank you to Auntie Ronyea, Uncle Ray, Auntie NiChelle, Uncle Michael, Uncle Scottie, Uncle Rob, cousins The Bryants, Willie, RaiDion, Ryleigh, and Robbie for loving us.

To my grandma, "GG" Author Jerri Lynn, for supporting us, spoiling us and teaching us how to be BIG little kids.

To my mommy, Author Tori Lynn, I LOVE YOU MOMMY!!!

Hey Kids,
We are little people but we have BIG feelings. Because we're little, sometimes big people forget to ask us how we feel. We would like them to ask but if the big people forget, then we can write or draw our feelings here.
It's okay to feel happy, sad, excited, angry, afraid or brave. IT'S OKAY!

Our Feelings Matter.

"Kids are people too, they are just in little bodies."
Mae H. Ponds

RIGHT ON GREAT-GRANDMA!!!

ARE YOU READY KIDS???

Ryan says, "My feelings matter because I am special, I have feelings, and I am a person even though I am little."

I am _____ and
My feelings matter
because

My feelings matter.

Today I feel...

Ryan says, "I am important because I am special. It is important for me to give and get hugs everyday.

Hugs make me feel good."

I ____ am important because

My feelings matter.
Today I feel...

Ryan says, "I am wonderful because I love myself, my family, and my teachers. Loving myself makes it easy to love others too."

I_____ am
wonderful because

My feelings matter.
Today I feel...

Ryan says, "I am okay because I lived in a homeless shelter. Living in a homeless shelter was hard, but, I decided to be happy anyway."

I _____ am
okay because

My feelings matter.
Today I feel...

Ryan says, "I feel safe because, my parent loves me, takes care of me, and won't let anything happen to me. Yes, that makes me feel safe."

I _____ am safe
because

My feelings matter.
Today I feel...

Ryan says, "I am brave because I stood up to a bully. I don't LET anyone bully me, but I don't bully others either. You can be brave too."

I_____ am
brave because

My feelings matter.
Today I feel...

Ryan says, "I am strong because I eat lots of fruits. I love to eat grapes, watermelon and strawberries. And, I like to run and play outside. I like to feel healthy."

I_____ am
strong because

My feelings matter.
Today I feel...

Ryan says, "I am proud because I pick out my own clothes all by myself. I like to wear bright colors. I feel proud when I dress myself."

I _____ am
proud because

My feelings matter.

Today I feel...

Ryan says, "I am smart because I love to learn. I love to read books. When I read it makes me feel smart."

I _____ am
smart because

My feelings matter.

Today I feel...

Ryan says, "I am fun because I love to be happy and be silly. I am fun because I love to play with other kids. And, I like to make people laugh."

I _____ am fun
because

My feelings matter.
Today I feel...

Ryan says, "I am getting better because I use to be really shy and wouldn't sing but everyday I am getting better and better. And, I am getting better at math."

I _____ am
getting better at

My feelings matter.
Today I feel...

Ryan says, "I am famous because one day I want to be on TV. When I get big, I am going to be a rock star or a Dr that fix animals."

I _____ am
famous because

My feelings matter.

Today I feel...

Ryan says, "I am amazing because if I get sad, it may be for a short while but I can make myself feel happy again if I read a book, play with my toys, or get a hug."

I_____ am
amazing because

My feelings matter.

Today I feel...

Ryan says, "I am talented because I can act, sing, dance, and create."

I _____ am
talented because

My feelings matter.
Today I feel...

Ryan says, "I am happy. What makes me happy is hearing the song "HAPPY" and dancing. Also hugs, kisses, reading, playing, and drawing makes me happy. Whenever I get sad, I do one of these to get happy again."

I _____ am
Happy. If I get sad
I do these things to
feel happy again...

My feelings matter.
Today I feel...

YEA KIDS!!!

REMEMBER YOUR FEELINGS

MATTER!

www.ingramcontent.com/pod-product-compliance
Lightning Source LLC
Chambersburg PA
CBHW071437040426
42445CB00012BA/1382